THEY WHISPERED
TO STAY ALIVE —

BRING US HOME

They Whispered
to Stay Alive ~
Bring Us Home

Mark Loring

River Sanctuary Publishing
P.O Box 1561
Felton, CA 95018
www.riversanctuarypublishing.com
Dedicated to the awakening of the New Earth

*For Patterson Avenue and the
twenty-seven first cousins*

INTRODUCTION

Several years ago, I began writing a novel that focused on the "unfinished business" of returning home. Some of the characters stayed with me long after I had stopped writing. I missed them when I could no longer feel their presence.

During a writing meditation I invited them to visit. Although none of the primary characters returned, a relative of theirs did. Her name was "Geneva Alberta Roy." I called her "Miss. Geneva" and she called me "Salt."

"Miss. Geneva" would often speak to me in a whisper. When I asked her about the whispering, she explained that the whisper was an "offering to a forced silence." Her grandmother, who was born a slave, believed there was no time for "wasted words." They were not allowed to speak at night. If voices were heard, there were beatings and even death. So, they whispered.

An involuntary silence brought them to
themselves and each other.
The world did not permit their voices.
Yet the silence knew that the whisper
held its own freedom.

The magic of who we are
was never intended for perfection.
There is no rest there.

Free of yesterday's breath.
I have let it go.
I have completed my time there.

When you come to the realization that
in fact you had been choosing—
you were making choices
even when you weren't,
it can make for difficult days.
When that war arrives,
allow forgiveness to lead you into battle.

We are imperfect miracles.

Leave room for new beginnings.

We have always been at war with someone.
And we know that the wars at home
are the most painful.

Yet, and still,
we remain many beautiful things.

From your construction
I will no longer build.

Had I chosen to live my life in the closet
hidden from the world,
and more importantly from myself,
I wouldn't be alive today.
It was a decision in which I said,
to a grave dug for me:
This is my time.
This is my life.
I belong to it.
And it to me.

In the same breath,
you tell me that you love me.
I accept not your words
based on your truth.
Knowing for myself,
that you created neither heaven nor hell.
I am responsible for my own life.
I have seen enough days to know this.
I belong to me.
And I shall live my life.
Surrounded by those
whose love isn't marred in fear.

Listening is a mighty force.
Being heard is healing.

Courage can be a lonely place.

I will no longer seek myself through you.
I can no longer be found there
and have chosen a new way home.

Life lived in the shadows yields a voice
known only to unheard whispers.
Let it be your highest calling
to not only find your voice.
Your center.
Your purpose.
Your intention.
Your meaning.
Your home.
Let them be known
by the very names
that you give them.

Many of us are holding
forgiveness for ransom.

Celebrate the small things,
the small victories.
So that you don't forget
that you are here.

Vulnerability deserves acknowledgment.
Not fearful indulgence,
but a gentle acceptance,
that life isn't always,
predictable or clear.

Being enough
cannot be found,
in someone else's mind.

Tell me about the places in you
that knows love.
Then we can talk about freedom.

It is serious business
when our children come to us,
pleading for their survival.

Hold on to what holds you.

Do you remember the place
where the words didn't own us?

Perhaps our most vital contribution
for the collective healing of all people
is a conscious intent
towards the sacred undertaking
of unwrapping the wounds
that divide and join us.

Help me to be here.
Not there.
Not before.
Right here.

Don't forget to play.

Lay them down
here on these pages.
There are no caged butterflies.
There is blooming in December.

Locate your knower.
The one free of any God.
It is imperative that you recognize
the call of your own name.

The overwhelming geography of anxiety
is the cruel competition that it creates
between everything and nothing.

Monsters of fear,
who bear no responsibility
for their own emptiness.
Resenting death in the face
of their own careless destruction.
Death squads of ignorance,
hate, and complacency.
We have long known the mockery,
the shame, the bleeding devastation…

—of it all.

I am here until I am there.

Be aware of the free man or woman,
who brings you their deaths.

Tell me how to love it when it cries.

If you end up in hell,
at least bring something back.
Do not waste your pain.

Vulnerability needn't become
one's burial ground.

Birth and death, we are.
What gifts do they bring
and to whom shall they serve?

Shame had convinced me
that only one memory was allowed.

Although we are apart,
your name is remembered here.

These words hold their testimony.
Whispers declared
in the huts of the ancestors
whose feet graced the soil
where life accepted its first breath.
I am of that beginning.
Beloved.
Still.

First and always,
you are wanted
and needed here.
Each of you.
Your presence
and your participation
in your story
is vital to its narration.
Your voice belongs here.
You are not a footnote
to anyone's telling.

We know where the graves are.
We have always known.

If I were there,
I would join you in silence.
Knowing that there are no words,
yet so many.
We would speak, even laugh,
then return to silence without hesitation.
Shifting between the moments
like ancient dancers.

When morning comes for itself.
Marching from Birmingham, Alabama,
to Birmingham, England.
Deserving of breath.
Kneeling for liberties.
Let me be amongst the woke.
Let me witness the calling for more.
For no more.

In our negotiations with peace,
we are asked to hold
uncertainty and beauty
in the same space.
It is possible.
As we wait
for further understanding,
let this be
a reminder of our grace.

Our better selves
are built and remembered
when we become still.

Perhaps grief
is the language
that returns us
to ourselves.

One cannot bypass grace,
in pursuit of peace.

The moment had arrived
where there were no mothers,
fathers, aunts, or uncles to call.
We were all that remained.

I wanted to discover words
that didn't leave me
stranded in my suffering.

What if I told you
you could call the search off?

safe
whole
enough

Children want to know
that they are beautiful.
I'm not talking about perfect teeth,
long legs, and camera-friendly looks.
Nor am I suggesting an overindulgence
of feel-good statements and platitudes.
I'm talking about the beauty that is found
in being told that you are possible from within.
Words that build their becoming.
Stories that assist in returning themselves
to themselves.
Their very own versions
of their very own magic.

During this time,
what stories can we tell our children
that don't rob them of their hope?

In the days to come
what will you tell yourself
when the mind begins to beg for more?
When the spaces have become cold.
Where in-here begs for out-there.
How will you speak to the time
and what will you tell it?
What grace have you written for yourself?

I am needed here in this moment.
Nothing else shall be asked of me.

About the Author

Mark Loring, lives in Santa Cruz, California, with his husband, Steven, of twenty-two years and their cats, Nina and Simone. *They Whispered To Stay Alive—Bring Us Home* is his second collection of poetry. His first book of poetry *The Soul's Collection: An Intimate Awakening* was published in 2011.

www.ingramcontent.com/pod-product-compliance
Lightning Source LLC
Chambersburg PA
CBHW060040050426
42448CB00012B/3085